THIS PLANNER

BELONGS TO

2022

January

mon	tue	wed	thu	fri	sat	sun
					1	2
3	4	5	6	7	8	9
10	11	12	13	14	15	16
17	18	19	20	21	22	23
24	25	26	27	28	29	30
31						

February

mon	tue	wed	thu	fri	sat	sun
	1	2	3	4	5	6
7	8	9	10	11	12	13
14	15	16	17	18	19	20
21	22	23	24	25	26	27
28						

March

mon	tue	wed	thu	fri	sat	sun
	1	2	3	4	5	6
7	8	9	10	11	12	13
14	15	16	17	18	19	20
21	22	23	24	25	26	27
28	29	30	31			

April

mon	tue	wed	thu	fri	sat	sun
				1	2	3
4	5	6	7	8	9	10
11	12	13	14	15	16	17
18	19	20	21	22	23	24
25	26	27	28	29	30	

May

mon	tue	wed	thu	fri	sat	sun
						1
2	3	4	5	6	7	8
9	10	11	12	13	14	15
16	17	18	19	20	21	22
23	24	25	26	27	28	29
30	31					

June

mon	tue	wed	thu	fri	sat	sun
		1	2	3	4	5
6	7	8	9	10	11	12
13	14	15	16	17	18	19
20	21	22	23	24	25	26
27	28	29	30			

July

mon	tue	wed	thu	fri	sat	sun
				1	2	3
4	5	6	7	8	9	10
11	12	13	14	15	16	17
18	19	20	21	22	23	24
25	26	27	28	29	30	31

August

mon	tue	wed	thu	fri	sat	sun
1	2	3	4	5	6	7
8	9	10	11	12	13	14
15	16	17	18	19	20	21
22	23	24	25	26	27	28
29	30	31				

September

mon	tue	wed	thu	fri	sat	sun
			1	2	3	4
5	6	7	8	9	10	11
12	13	14	15	16	17	18
19	20	21	22	23	24	25
26	27	28	29	30		

October

mon	tue	wed	thu	fri	sat	sun
					1	2
3	4	5	6	7	8	9
10	11	12	13	14	15	16
17	18	19	20	21	22	23
24	25	26	27	28	29	30
31						

November

mon	tue	wed	thu	fri	sat	sun
	1	2	3	4	5	6
7	8	9	10	11	12	13
14	15	16	17	18	19	20
21	22	23	24	25	26	27
28	29	30				

December

mon	tue	wed	thu	fri	sat	sun
			1	2	3	4
5	6	7	8	9	10	11
12	13	14	15	16	17	18
19	20	21	22	23	24	25
26	27	28	29	30	31	

January

mon	tue	wed	thu	fri	sat	sun

Important

- ☐ ______________________________
- ☐ ______________________________
- ☐ ______________________________
- ☐ ______________________________
- ☐ ______________________________
- ☐ ______________________________

To buy

- ☐ ______________________________
- ☐ ______________________________
- ☐ ______________________________
- ☐ ______________________________
- ☐ ______________________________
- ☐ ______________________________

Notes

Week ___

Goals

- [ ]
- [ ]
- [ ]
- [ ]

monday	tuesday

wedneday	thursday

friday	saturday

sunday	Notes

In this week.....................

Expenses

Goals

Habits

I am grateful

Notes

Week ___

Goals

- [ ] _______________________
- [ ] _______________________
- [ ] _______________________
- [ ] _______________________

monday	tuesday

wedneday	thursday

friday	saturday

sunday	Notes

In this week.........................

Expenses

Goals

Habits

I am grateful

Notes

Week __

Goals

- [ ] ____________________
- [ ] ____________________
- [ ] ____________________
- [ ] ____________________

monday	tuesday
wedneday	**thursday**
friday	**saturday**
sunday	**Notes**

In this week.......................

Expenses

Goals

Habits

I am grateful

Notes

Week ___

Goals

- [ ]
- [ ]
- [ ]
- [ ]

monday	tuesday

wedneday	thursday

friday	saturday

sunday	Notes

In this week.....................

Expenses

Goals

Habits

I am grateful

Notes

Week ___

Goals

- [ ]
- [ ]
- [ ]
- [ ]

monday	tuesday

wedneday	thursday

friday	saturday

sunday	Notes

In this week.....................

Expenses

Goals

Habits

I am grateful

Notes

February

mon	tue	wed	thu	fri	sat	sun

Important

- ☐ _______________
- ☐ _______________
- ☐ _______________
- ☐ _______________
- ☐ _______________
- ☐ _______________

To buy

- ☐ _______________
- ☐ _______________
- ☐ _______________
- ☐ _______________
- ☐ _______________
- ☐ _______________

Notes

Week ___

Goals

- [ ] _______________________________
- [ ] _______________________________
- [ ] _______________________________
- [ ] _______________________________

monday	tuesday

wedneday	thursday

friday	saturday

sunday	Notes

In this week.............................

Expenses

Goals

Habits

I am grateful

Notes

Week ____

Goals

- ☐ __________________________
- ☐ __________________________
- ☐ __________________________
- ☐ __________________________

monday	tuesday

wedneday	thursday

friday	saturday

sunday	Notes

In this week......................

Expenses

Goals

Habits

I am grateful

Notes

Week ___

Goals

- [ ]
- [ ]
- [ ]
- [ ]

monday	tuesday

wmedneday	thursday

friday	saturday

sunday	Notes

In this week.....................

Expenses

Goals

Habits

I am grateful

Notes

Week ___

Goals

- [ ] ____
- [ ] ____
- [ ] ____
- [ ] ____

monday	tuesday

wedneday	thursday

friday	saturday

sunday	Notes

In this week...............

Expenses

Goals

Habits

I am grateful

Notes

Week ___

Goals

- [ ] _______________________________
- [ ] _______________________________
- [ ] _______________________________
- [ ] _______________________________

monday	tuesday

wedneday	thursday

friday	saturday

sunday	Notes

In this week...................

Expenses

Goals

Habits

I am grateful

Notes

March

mon	tue	wed	thu	fri	sat	sun

Important

- [ ] _______________________
- [ ] _______________________
- [ ] _______________________
- [ ] _______________________
- [ ] _______________________
- [ ] _______________________

To buy

- [ ] _______________________
- [ ] _______________________
- [ ] _______________________
- [ ] _______________________
- [ ] _______________________
- [ ] _______________________

Notes

Week ___

Goals

- ☐ ________________________
- ☐ ________________________
- ☐ ________________________
- ☐ ________________________

| monday | tuesday |

| wedneday | thursday |

| friday | saturday |

| sunday | Notes |

In this week.........................

Expenses

Goals

Habits

I am grateful

Notes

Week ___

Goals

- [ ] ______________________
- [ ] ______________________
- [ ] ______________________
- [ ] ______________________

monday	tuesday

wedneday	thursday

friday	saturday

sunday	Notes

In this week...........................

Expenses

Goals

Habits

I am grateful

Notes

Week ___

Goals

- [ ] ______________________
- [ ] ______________________
- [ ] ______________________
- [ ] ______________________

monday	tuesday

wednesday	thursday

friday	saturday

sunday	Notes

In this week.....................

Expenses

Goals

Habits

I am grateful

Notes

Week ____

Goals

- [ ] _______________________________
- [ ] _______________________________
- [ ] _______________________________
- [ ] _______________________________

monday	tuesday

wmedneday	thursday

friday	saturday

sunday	Notes

In this week................

Expenses

Goals

Habits

I am grateful

Notes

Week ___

Goals

- [ ]
- [ ]
- [ ]
- [ ]

monday	tuesday

wedneday	thursday

friday	saturday

sunday	Notes

In this week.....................

Expenses

Goals

Habits

I am grateful

Notes

April

mon	tue	wed	thu	fri	sat	sun

Important

- [ ] _______________________
- [ ] _______________________
- [ ] _______________________
- [ ] _______________________
- [ ] _______________________
- [ ] _______________________

To buy

- [ ] _______________________
- [ ] _______________________
- [ ] _______________________
- [ ] _______________________
- [ ] _______________________
- [ ] _______________________

Notes

Week ___

Goals

- [ ]
- [ ]
- [ ]
- [ ]

monday	tuesday

wedneday	thursday

friday	saturday

sunday	Notes

In this week.....................

Expenses

Goals

Habits

I am grateful

Notes

Week ___

Goals

- [ ]
- [ ]
- [ ]
- [ ]

| monday | tuesday |

| wedneday | thursday |

| friday | saturday |

| sunday | Notes |

In this week..................

Expenses

Goals

Habits

I am grateful

Notes

Week ___

Goals

- [ ]
- [ ]
- [ ]
- [ ]

monday	tuesday
wedneday	thursday
friday	saturday
sunday	Notes

In this week.........................

Expenses

Goals

Habits

I am grateful

Notes

Week ___

Goals

- [ ] ________________________
- [ ] ________________________
- [ ] ________________________
- [ ] ________________________

monday

tuesday

wedneday

thursday

friday

saturday

sunday

Notes

In this week.........................

Expenses

Goals

Habits

I am grateful

Notes

Week ___

Goals

- [ ] ___________________________________
- [ ] ___________________________________
- [ ] ___________________________________
- [ ] ___________________________________

monday	tuesday

wedneday	thursday

friday	saturday

sunday	Notes

In this week........................

Expenses

Goals

Habits

I am grateful

Notes

May

mon	tue	wed	thu	fri	sat	sun

Important

- ☐ _______________
- ☐ _______________
- ☐ _______________
- ☐ _______________
- ☐ _______________
- ☐ _______________

To buy

- ☐ _______________
- ☐ _______________
- ☐ _______________
- ☐ _______________
- ☐ _______________
- ☐ _______________

Notes

Week ___

Goals

- [ ] _________________________
- [ ] _________________________
- [ ] _________________________
- [ ] _________________________

monday	tuesday

wedneday	thursday

friday	saturday

sunday	Notes

In this week...................

Expenses

Goals

Habits

I am grateful

Notes

Week ___

Goals

- [ ]
- [ ]
- [ ]
- [ ]

monday	tuesday

wedneday	thursday

friday	saturday

sunday	Notes

In this week.....................

Expenses

Goals

Habits

I am grateful

Notes

Week ___

Goals

- [ ]
- [ ]
- [ ]
- [ ]

monday	tuesday

wedneday	thursday

friday	saturday

sunday	Notes

In this week.......................

Expenses

Goals

Habits

I am grateful

Notes

Week ___

Goals

- [ ]
- [ ]
- [ ]
- [ ]

monday	tuesday
wedneday	thursday
friday	saturday
sunday	Notes

In this week...................

Expenses

Goals

Habits

I am grateful

Notes

Week ___

Goals

- [ ] ________________________________
- [ ] ________________________________
- [ ] ________________________________
- [ ] ________________________________

monday	tuesday

wchneday	thursday

friday	saturday

sunday	Notes

In this week.......................

Expenses

Goals

Habits

I am grateful

Notes

June

mon	tue	wed	thu	fri	sat	sun

Important

- ☐ __________________________
- ☐ __________________________
- ☐ __________________________
- ☐ __________________________
- ☐ __________________________
- ☐ __________________________

To buy

- ☐ __________________________
- ☐ __________________________
- ☐ __________________________
- ☐ __________________________
- ☐ __________________________
- ☐ __________________________

Notes

Week ___

Goals

- [ ]
- [ ]
- [ ]
- [ ]

monday	tuesday

wedneday	thursday

friday	saturday

sunday	Notes

In this week..........................

Expenses

Goals

Habits

I am grateful

Notes

Week ___

Goals

- [ ] ______________________________
- [ ] ______________________________
- [ ] ______________________________
- [ ] ______________________________

monday	tuesday

wedneday	thursday

friday	saturday

sunday	Notes

In this week...........................

Expenses

Goals

Habits

I am grateful

Notes

Week ___

Goals

- [ ]
- [ ]
- [ ]
- [ ]

monday	tuesday

wedneday	thursday

friday	saturday

sunday	Notes

In this week.........................

Expenses

Goals

Habits

I am grateful

Notes

Week ___

Goals

- [ ]
- [ ]
- [ ]
- [ ]

| monday | tuesday |

| wedneday | thursday |

| friday | saturday |

| sunday | Notes |

In this week.....................

Expenses

Goals

Habits

I am grateful

Notes

Week ___

Goals

- [ ] _______________________________________
- [ ] _______________________________________
- [ ] _______________________________________
- [ ] _______________________________________

monday	tuesday

wedneday	thursday

friday	saturday

sunday	Notes

In this week.........................

Expenses

Goals

Habits

I am grateful

Notes

July

mon	tue	wed	thu	fri	sat	sun

Important

- ☐ ______________________
- ☐ ______________________
- ☐ ______________________
- ☐ ______________________
- ☐ ______________________
- ☐ ______________________

To buy

- ☐ ______________________
- ☐ ______________________
- ☐ ______________________
- ☐ ______________________
- ☐ ______________________
- ☐ ______________________

Notes

Week ___

Goals

- [ ] _______________________________________
- [ ] _______________________________________
- [ ] _______________________________________
- [ ] _______________________________________

monday	tuesday

wedneday	thursday

friday	saturday

sunday	Notes

In this week.........................

Expenses

Goals

Habits

I am grateful

Notes

Week ___

Goals

- [ ]
- [ ]
- [ ]
- [ ]

monday	tuesday

wmedneday	thursday

friday	saturday

sunday	Notes

In this week.............................

Expenses

Goals

Habits

I am grateful

Notes

Week ___

Goals

- [ ]
- [ ]
- [ ]
- [ ]

monday	tuesday

wedneday	thursday

friday	saturday

sunday	Notes

In this week.....................

Expenses

Goals

Habits

I am grateful

Notes

Week ___

Goals

- [ ]
- [ ]
- [ ]
- [ ]

| monday | tuesday |

| wedneday | thursday |

| friday | saturday |

| sunday | Notes |

In this week......................

Expenses

Goals

Habits

I am grateful

Notes

Week___

Goals

- ☐ _______________________
- ☐ _______________________
- ☐ _______________________
- ☐ _______________________

monday	tuesday

wedneday	thursday

friday	saturday

sunday	Notes

In this week.....................

Expenses

Goals

Habits

I am grateful

Notes

August

mon	tue	wed	thu	fri	sat	sun

Important

- ☐ _______________________
- ☐ _______________________
- ☐ _______________________
- ☐ _______________________
- ☐ _______________________
- ☐ _______________________

To buy

- ☐ _______________________
- ☐ _______________________
- ☐ _______________________
- ☐ _______________________
- ☐ _______________________
- ☐ _______________________

Notes

Week ___

Goals

- [ ] ______________________________
- [ ] ______________________________
- [ ] ______________________________
- [ ] ______________________________

monday	tuesday

wedneday	thursday

friday	saturday

sunday	Notes

In this week............................

Expenses

Goals

Habits

I am grateful

Notes

Week ___

Goals

- [ ]
- [ ]
- [ ]
- [ ]

monday	tuesday

wedneday	thursday

friday	saturday

sunday	Notes

In this week.....................

Expenses

Goals

Habits

I am grateful

Notes

Week ___

Goals

- [ ]
- [ ]
- [ ]
- [ ]

| monday | tuesday |

| wedneday | thursday |

| friday | saturday |

| sunday | Notes |

In this week............................

Expenses

Goals

Habits

I am grateful

Notes

Week ___

Goals

- [ ]
- [ ]
- [ ]
- [ ]

| monday | tuesday |

| wedneday | thursday |

| friday | saturday |

| sunday | Notes |

In this week.........................

Expenses

Goals

Habits

I am grateful

Notes

Week ___

Goals

- [ ] ________________________________
- [ ] ________________________________
- [ ] ________________________________
- [ ] ________________________________

monday	tuesday
wedneday	**thursday**
friday	**saturday**
sunday	**Notes**

In this week...........................

Expenses

Goals

Habits

I am grateful

Notes

September

mon	tue	wed	thu	fri	sat	sun

Important

- [ ] ___________________________
- [ ] ___________________________
- [ ] ___________________________
- [ ] ___________________________
- [ ] ___________________________
- [ ] ___________________________

To buy

- [ ] ___________________________
- [ ] ___________________________
- [ ] ___________________________
- [ ] ___________________________
- [ ] ___________________________
- [ ] ___________________________

Notes

Week ___

Goals

- [ ] ________________
- [ ] ________________
- [ ] ________________
- [ ] ________________

monday	tuesday

wedneday	thursday

friday	saturday

sunday	Notes

In this week...................

Expenses

Goals

Habits

I am grateful

Notes

Week ___

Goals

- [ ]
- [ ]
- [ ]
- [ ]

monday	tuesday

wedneday	thursday

friday	saturday

sunday	Notes

In this week........................

Expenses

Goals

Habits

I am grateful

Notes

Week ___

Goals

- [ ]
- [ ]
- [ ]
- [ ]

monday	tuesday

wedneday	thursday

friday	saturday

sunday	Notes

In this week.........................

Expenses

Goals

Habits

I am grateful

Notes

Week ___

Goals

- [ ] ________________________
- [ ] ________________________
- [ ] ________________________
- [ ] ________________________

| monday | tuesday |

| wedneday | thursday |

| friday | saturday |

| sunday | Notes |

In this week...................

Expenses

Goals

Habits

I am grateful

Notes

Week ___

Goals

- [ ]
- [ ]
- [ ]
- [ ]

| monday | tuesday |

| wedneday | thursday |

| friday | saturday |

| sunday | Notes |

In this week.....................

Expenses

Goals

Habits

I am grateful

Notes

October

mon	tue	wed	thu	fri	sat	sun

Important

- ☐ ______________________
- ☐ ______________________
- ☐ ______________________
- ☐ ______________________
- ☐ ______________________
- ☐ ______________________

To buy

- ☐ ______________________
- ☐ ______________________
- ☐ ______________________
- ☐ ______________________
- ☐ ______________________
- ☐ ______________________

Notes

Week ___

Goals

- [ ] ________________________
- [ ] ________________________
- [ ] ________________________
- [ ] ________________________

monday	tuesday

wedneday	thursday

friday	saturday

sunday	Notes

In this week........................

Expenses

Goals

Habits

I am grateful

Notes

Week ___

Goals

- [ ] ____
- [ ] ____
- [ ] ____
- [ ] ____

monday	tuesday

wedneday	thursday

friday	saturday

sunday	Notes

In this week.........................

Expenses

Goals

Habits

I am grateful

Notes

Week ___

Goals

- ☐ ________________________
- ☐ ________________________
- ☐ ________________________
- ☐ ________________________

monday	tuesday

wedneday	thursday

friday	saturday

sunday	Notes

In this week...................

Expenses

Goals

Habits

I am grateful

Notes

Week ___

Goals

- [ ] _______________________________
- [ ] _______________________________
- [ ] _______________________________
- [ ] _______________________________

monday	tuesday

wedneday	thursday

friday	saturday

sunday	Notes

In this week....................

Expenses

Goals

Habits

I am grateful

Notes

Week ___

Goals

- [ ] ____
- [ ] ____
- [ ] ____
- [ ] ____

monday	tuesday

wedneday	thursday

friday	saturday

sunday	Notes

In this week.......................

Expenses

Goals

Habits

I am grateful

Notes

November

mon	tue	wed	thu	fri	sat	sun

Important

- ☐ ____________________
- ☐ ____________________
- ☐ ____________________
- ☐ ____________________
- ☐ ____________________
- ☐ ____________________

To buy

- ☐ ____________________
- ☐ ____________________
- ☐ ____________________
- ☐ ____________________
- ☐ ____________________
- ☐ ____________________

Notes

Week ___

Goals

- ☐ ________________________________
- ☐ ________________________________
- ☐ ________________________________
- ☐ ________________________________

| monday | tuesday |

| wedneday | thursday |

| friday | saturday |

| sunday | Notes |

In this week......................

Expenses

Goals

Habits

I am grateful

Notes

Week ___

Goals

- [ ]
- [ ]
- [ ]
- [ ]

monday	tuesday

wedneday	thursday

friday	saturday

sunday	Notes

In this week.....................

Expenses

Goals

Habits

I am grateful

Notes

Week ___

Goals

- [ ] ______________________
- [ ] ______________________
- [ ] ______________________
- [ ] ______________________

monday	tuesday

wedneday	thursday

friday	saturday

sunday	Notes

In this week...................

Expenses

Goals

Habits

I am grateful

Notes

Week ___

Goals

- [ ]
- [ ]
- [ ]
- [ ]

monday	tuesday

wedneday	thursday

friday	saturday

sunday	Notes

In this week..........................

Expenses

Goals

Habits

I am grateful

Notes

Week ___

Goals

- ☐ ____
- ☐ ____
- ☐ ____
- ☐ ____

monday	tuesday

wedneday	thursday

friday	saturday

sunday	Notes

In this week.....................

Expenses

Goals

Habits

I am grateful

Notes

December

mon	tue	wed	thu	fri	sat	sun

Important

- ☐ ________________________
- ☐ ________________________
- ☐ ________________________
- ☐ ________________________
- ☐ ________________________
- ☐ ________________________

To buy

- ☐ ________________________
- ☐ ________________________
- ☐ ________________________
- ☐ ________________________
- ☐ ________________________
- ☐ ________________________

Notes

Week ___

Goals

- [ ] ______________________________
- [ ] ______________________________
- [ ] ______________________________
- [ ] ______________________________

monday	tuesday

wmedneday	thursday

friday	saturday

sunday	Notes

In this week..........................

Expenses

Goals

Habits

I am grateful

Notes

Week ___

Goals

- [ ] ______________________
- [ ] ______________________
- [ ] ______________________
- [ ] ______________________

| monday | tuesday |

| wedneday | thursday |

| friday | saturday |

| sunday | Notes |

In this week........................

Expenses

Goals

Habits

I am grateful

Notes

Week ___

Goals

- [ ] ______________________________
- [ ] ______________________________
- [ ] ______________________________
- [ ] ______________________________

monday	tuesday

wedneday	thursday

friday	saturday

sunday	Notes

In this week.........................

Expenses

Goals

Habits

I am grateful

Notes

Week ___

Goals

- [ ] _______________________________________
- [ ] _______________________________________
- [ ] _______________________________________
- [ ] _______________________________________

monday	tuesday
wedneday	thursday
friday	saturday
sunday	Notes

In this week.......................

Expenses

Goals

Habits

I am grateful

Notes

Week ___

Goals

- ☐ _______________
- ☐ _______________
- ☐ _______________
- ☐ _______________

monday

tuesday

wedneday

thursday

friday

saturday

sunday

Notes

In this week...........................

Expenses

Goals

Habits

I am grateful

Notes

Notes

Notes

Notes

Notes

Notes

Notes